In the dining room Mom was looking at Gramma's shelves of special things. Gramma has lots of knickknacks all over the house, little statues and pitchers and silver things. Mom says they're valuable. They are certainly pretty.

"Where's the little owl?" asked Mom. She pointed to the spot where a little owl statue usually sat. I liked the owl because he had little silver feet and big silver eyes. He stood on a piece of fancy stone.

"Sh," said Grampa. "Gramma moved it and can't remember where she put it. If we talk about it, she gets upset."

"Maybe I can find it, Grampa," I said.

"That's a great idea," Grampa said.

"What's a great idea?" asked Gramma as she came into the room.

"I'm going to find the owl you lost," I said.

THE ADVENTURES OF
SCOOTER and JAKE
Whoo Done It?

Gayle Roper

CHARIOT
FAMILY
PUBLISHING
A DIVISION OF COOK COMMUNICATIONS

Chariot Family Publishing
Cook Communications, Colorado Springs, CO 80918
Cook Communications, Paris, Ontario
Kingsway Communications, Eastbourne, England

WHOO DONE IT?
© 1996 by Gayle Roper for text and J. Steven Hunt for illustrations

Cover design by Joe Ragont
Cover illustration by J. Steven Hunt
First printing, 1996
Printed in The United States of America
00 99 98 97 96   5 4 3 2 1

Table of Contents

Chapter One 7

Chapter Two 10

Chapter Three 13

Chapter Four 16

Chapter Five 18

Chapter Six 21

Chapter Seven 24

Chapter Eight 27

Chapter Nine 30

Chapter Ten 32

Chapter Eleven 36

Chapter Twelve 39

Chapter Thirteen 42

Chapter Fourteen 44

Chapter Fifteen 47

CHAPTER 1

When we turned onto Paris Avenue, I looked out the window. I wanted to be the first to see Grampa and Gramma's house.

"I see it!" yelled Jake. "There it is!"

"You don't have to scream in my ear," I said. "We can all hear you." I was sad that Jake saw the house first.

Jake is my eight-year-old sister, and she's in third grade. Her real name is Jacqueline Anne, but we call her Jake. I'm Scooter. I'm seven and in second grade. My real name is Ryan Jeffrey Grady, but no one calls me that.

As soon as Dad pulled up at Grampa and Gramma's house, the front door opened. Grampa and Gramma Grady came out and smiled and waved. Their dog, Old Henry, came out with them.

Grampa and Gramma are really our great-grandparents. They are very old. Grampa is eighty and Gramma is seventy-eight. Grampa doesn't have much hair any more, just a fringe around the edges. Gramma has curly white hair that's fluffy and pretty. Both of them have lots of wrinkles. Their skin looks like Dad's shirts before they get ironed.

Old Henry is very old too. He is a yellow cocker spaniel—at least he used to be yellow. Now he's turning gray like Grampa. Old Henry has no energy anymore. He just lies around all day.

Jake and I ran up the walk. We love to come to Grampa and Gramma's house. It's fun to go where people love you a lot.

Gramma and Grampa let us do special things like stay up late if we want to. Sometimes we fall asleep on the living room sofa watching TV. When Gramma and Grampa go to bed, they wake us up.

"Come on, sweethearts," Gramma says. "Time to go upstairs."

All four of us go up together. We all brush our teeth and put on our pajamas, only Gramma wears a nightie. Then Grampa prays for all of us.

"Dear God," he says, "thanks for Scooter and Jake. We love them and You love them. Help them sleep tight. And help Gramma and me sleep tight too. Help us always to do good to all."

I try not to fall asleep while he prays, but sometimes it's hard. Then we all sleep until we feel like getting up.

This trip we were going to stay at Gramma and Grampa's for the weekend while Mom and Dad went on a little vacation.

"Here are my sweethearts!" Gramma said as she kissed us. "Do I have some special things for you!"

"What?" we asked. Gramma always made wonderful goodies just for Jake and me. We all went into the house and straight to the kitchen.

"This bag's for you," Gramma said to Jake. Inside Jake's plastic bag were wonderful chocolate chip cookies.

"My favorite!" Jake gave Gramma a hug.

"And this bag is for you, Scooter." She handed me a plastic bag full of snickerdoodles, my favorites.

"I'm so glad you're here," said Grampa. He smiled at Jake and me.

We smiled back. "So are we."

CHAPTER 2

Jake and I helped Dad carry our gym bags into the house. I put mine in the room that was always mine. It had been my grandfather's when he was a little boy, then my dad's when he visited. Now it's mine.

I ran downstairs and out to the back yard. Grampa had a birdbath that sat on a tree stump. Every day he washed it out with an old scrub brush. Then he poured in fresh water. I helped him pour the water. We poured a little extra in a bowl for Old Henry.

"Come on, Scooter," Grampa said. "Sit with me and watch the birds play."

We sat very still. Soon a pair of birds came to the birdbath and started dancing in the water. They flapped their wings. They put their beaks down for a drink. The water drops sparkled in the sunshine.

"I love God's birds," said Grampa.

"Did Old Henry chase them when he was a puppy?" I asked.

Grampa nodded. "Now he just ignores them."

"Come for dinner," called Gramma from the back door.

In the dining room Mom was looking at Gramma's shelves of special things. Gramma has lots of knickknacks all over the house, little statues and pitchers and silver things. Mom says they're valuable. They are certainly pretty.

"Where's the little owl?" asked Mom. She pointed to the spot where a little owl statue usually sat. I liked the owl because he had little silver feet and big silver eyes. He stood on a piece of fancy stone.

"Sh," said Grampa. "Gramma moved it, and now she can't remember where she put it. If I ask her about it, she gets upset."

"Maybe I can find it, Grampa," I said.

"That's a great idea," Grampa said.

"What's a great idea?" asked Gramma as she came into the room.

"I'm going to find the owl you lost," I said.

"I didn't lose it," said Gramma. "He did." She pointed to Grampa. "He doesn't remember where he put it, so he blames me. Now let's sit down for dinner."

CHAPTER 3

We had spaghetti for dinner. Gramma makes the best spaghetti in the world. She doesn't pour it from bottles or defrost it or anything. She cooks it in a big pan on her stove all day.

Grampa prayed for the meal. Grampa loves to pray, and I love to hear him.

"Dear God," he said, "I'm so glad to have our family visiting. Take very good care of Scooter and Jake. Help them and the rest of us always to do good to all. And thank You for this delicious spaghetti!"

When we finished the spaghetti, Mom took the dirty plates away. Old Henry waddled after her, hoping for some leftovers. Gramma carried in a huge chocolate cake.

"I made this for you," she said to my father.

Dad smiled. "My favorite!"

"Ever since he was a little boy, he's liked this

cake," Gramma said to Jake and me.

Gramma serves us this cake every time we come. I'm glad Dad liked it when he was a boy. I like it too.

One of my favorite things at Grampa and Gramma's is the special tablecloth Jake and I can color on. We sit at the table and draw people and houses and trees and anything we want. Then we erase and start over again. There's something real fun about drawing on a tablecloth.

After I finished my cake, I reached over to the little shelf beside the table. I grabbed my special crayons. I took one out and drew a circle around my empty plate. Then I drew a bigger circle and a bigger and a bigger. Soon I had a bunch of circles that spilled over onto the tablecloth in front of Jake.

"That's very nice, Scooter," said Grampa. "But stay in front of your place."

I grinned and took the blackboard eraser he handed to me. I erased all my circles. Then I pushed my plate out of the way and drew a rainbow.

Soon it was time to say good-bye to Mom and Dad.

"Have a good time on your vacation," said Grampa. "We'll take good care of these two."

I always feel a little funny when Mom and Dad go away, but I get over it fast, especially at Gramma and Grampa's.

The four of us and Old Henry settled back to watch some TV. We laughed a lot, and it got later and later. Gramma and Grampa made believe they didn't notice. Jake and I made believe we weren't yawning. Old Henry snored.

"How about some popcorn?" asked Gramma. She and Jake went to the kitchen and came back soon with a bowl of popcorn all steamy and warm. Old Henry even woke up long enough to eat some.

CHAPTER 4

During a commercial, I looked at the wall.

"Grampa," I said. I pointed to a group of pictures. "Where's the owl that used to hang there?"

"What do you mean, Scooter?" Grampa asked. "The wall is full of owls."

And it was. There were paintings of owls. There were photographs of owls. There was an owl that Mom had sewn for Gramma. There was an owl carved out of wood and sitting on a real branch. There was an owl drawn with ink.

But there should have been one more owl, my favorite.

"Where's the owl made of pinecone pieces and seeds?"

I liked this owl because all his feathers were little pieces of pinecone. I always wondered how long it had taken someone to take a pinecone apart and glue each little piece in place.

"Why, it is missing," said Gramma. She got up and walked to the wall. "Did you knock it down and break it?" she asked Grampa.

He got up and stood beside her. "I most certainly did not," he said.

"You must have," said Gramma. "It's gone."

Grampa looked upset. "I didn't, Lottie. Honest."

Gramma looked upset. "You just don't remember," she said.

Grampa looked at Old Henry, asleep under the end table. "It must have been the dog," he said, trying to make a joke.

Gramma took his hand. "It's okay," she said. "We'll find it."

But we all knew it wasn't okay. We all knew that it was a bad thing when an old person couldn't remember doing things.

CHAPTER 5

The next morning Jake and I went downstairs and watched Saturday cartoons on TV. Mom doesn't let us watch TV too much, but Gramma says, "It's okay while they're here. It's their vacation."

After breakfast Freddie came. Freddie is Gramma and Grampa's handyman. He comes every Tuesday, Thursday, and Saturday morning.

Freddie does all kinds of jobs that Grampa and Gramma can't do for themselves anymore. He cuts the grass. He washes the windows. He takes care of the garden. He does some cleaning. He paints and repairs and fixes broken things. In the winter he shovels snow.

I found Freddie in the back hall by the closet.

"Hey, Freddie!" I yelled.

I startled him, and he jumped. He also dropped something that crashed and clanged.

I watched as he picked up a big silver pitcher of Gramma's from the floor. He set it on the top shelf

of the closet.

"Hey, Scooter," he said, smiling. "I didn't know you were coming for a visit."

"Gramma and Grampa wanted to surprise you," I said.

"Well, they sure did!" Freddie closed the closet door.

"What are we doing today?" I asked Freddie. He lets us help him with his jobs.

"Why don't we pull the weeds in the back garden?" he asked. "Then we can water the flowers."

"Sounds good to me," I said.

"Scooter. Scooter. Come here a minute." It was Gramma calling me from the cellar.

"Go see what she wants," Freddie said. "Then you can help me."

I found Gramma by the dryer.

"Will you carry these clothes upstairs for me?" she asked. She pointed to a full laundry basket. "You have a young back and strong arms."

I picked up the laundry and carefully went upstairs. Then I went looking for Freddie. I found him leaning out the window in the dining room.

Freddie is a funny little man. His body looks like a skinny kid, but his face looks like a sad man. He is always very nice to everyone.

Freddie closed the dining room window and we went outside. I pulled weeds and watered flowers with Freddie until it was time for him to leave.

I walked down the street with him. He just lives around the corner.

"Freddie," I said. "Do Gramma and Grampa forget things very often?"

"Sometimes," Freddie said. "Last week they forgot to go to the doctor's."

"Do they misplace things?" I asked.

"Why?" Freddie looked at me. "Can't you find your snickerdoodles?"

"If they were lost," I said, "it would be my father who took them. He loves to eat them."

Freddie laughed at the idea of my father taking my cookies. Then he got serious. "Don't worry yourself about your grandma and grandpa," he said. "They're doing just fine. I'm taking good care of them."

I felt good that they had Freddie.

CHAPTER 6

After Freddie left, I sat down with my snickerdoodles and tried to think. Where would Grampa put something? I hide my special things in my bedroom. Maybe Grampa did too.

I went upstairs and stood in the door to Grampa's room. He has his own room across the hall from Gramma.

"He snores so loudly that I had to put him across the hall," said Gramma. "I need my beauty sleep, you know."

Grampa had a big bureau along one wall. Maybe the picture and the little owl were on the top.

If they were, I would never find them. I couldn't see that high.

I looked around. There was a chair by the bed. I pulled it and pushed it until I got it beside the bureau. Then I climbed up.

The top of Grampa's bureau was full of things.

There were dollar bills and dimes and quarters.
There were notes from Gramma and forms from the
doctor. There were three hankies. There was a
necktie folded in half. There was a picture of
Grampa and Old Henry when he was Young Henry.
There was a bottle of pills. There were car keys and
an old battery and deodorant.

The missing things weren't there.

I climbed down from my chair. I went to the
little table beside his bed. There I found a clock
radio and a box of tissues and an extra pair of
glasses. There was a picture of Gramma when she
was a girl. There were two books and a Bible.
Grampa loves to read his Bible.

There was no little owl with silver feet, and no
owl made of pine cone pieces.

I went to his chair by the window. Grampa keeps
his chess set there. He had the board set up with
figures made of wood. They were pretty pieces, but
I liked the pieces made of polished stone better.
Some of them were black and some were white, and
they were all carved in fancy shapes. I liked to play
soldiers with them.

I pulled open the drawer to get the stone pieces
out. They weren't there. I went to the stairs and

called to Grampa.

"Where are your stone chessmen?" I asked.
"I want to play soldiers."

"In the drawer in the table by the window," he called back. "Come on down now. We're going to drive to the lake so Old Henry can take his run."

"Be right there," I called.

Before I ran downstairs, I went back to Grampa's table. I searched the drawer again. The stone chessmen were not there.

CHAPTER 7

Jake and I climbed into the back seat of Grampa's car with Old Henry. Old Henry looked surprised to have company.

"Don't worry, Old Henry," I said. "There's plenty of room for all of us."

Gramma and Grampa sat in the front seat.

"Turn left here, dear," Gramma said. "Now turn right. And turn left at the stop sign."

I looked at Jake and grinned. Gramma always gives Grampa directions, and he listens for a while. Then he gets mad.

"The light is red," Gramma said. "Be sure to stop."

Grampa got mad. "My dear," he said. "I am not color blind. I can tell a red light. And I have not lost my mind. I know the way to the lake. I've been driving there for years."

Gramma was upset. "Oh, dear," she said. "I've

24

been bossy again. I'm sorry."

She was quiet for two blocks. Then she couldn't stand it any longer.

"There's the parking lot, my dear," she said. "You'd better pull in."

Jake and I climbed out of the car. I held the door for Old Henry. He stood at the edge of the back seat and looked at the ground. It must have looked very far away to him. I picked him up and lifted him out.

"He's heavy!" I said as I put him down.

"Gramma feeds him too much," said Grampa.

"I don't know, Grampa," said Jake. "It's you he sits beside at meals. I think you're the one who gives him scraps."

We walked slowly to the lake. Old Henry would take a few steps, then rest, take a few steps, then rest. When we got to the water, Old Henry lay down, all worn out.

Gramma gave Jake and me the bag of old bread she had brought.

"Feed the ducks, sweethearts," she said.

We tore off bits of bread and threw them into the water. Soon we were surrounded by ducks and geese.

One of the ducks kept nipping at my shoe if I

didn't feed him fast enough.

"Take it easy," I told him. "I'll feed you. But you have to share."

He bit my shoe again. He didn't want to share.

Soon Grampa said, "Old Henry's tired. We'd better go home."

When we got

back to the house, it was a happy surprise to see Freddie working on the hedge out front.

CHAPTER 8

"Hey, Freddie," I called as I jumped out of the car.

"Hey, Scooter. Hey, Jake." He smiled at us. He left the hedge and walked to the car. He had his workbag hung over his arm as usual. He uses it to carry his tools and cloths and things for his jobs.

"Is everything all right?" asked Gramma. She looked worried.

"Everything's fine," said Freddie. "I just wanted to be certain I had turned the hose off."

He waved good-bye and went home again.

Old Henry walked very slowly to the house, and we all went in. Old Henry collapsed in the front hall. He was all worn out from his adventure. I didn't think he would move again all day.

"Do you want some milk to go with your cookies?" Gramma asked Jake and me.

"Oh, yes," we both said. Watching the ducks eat

had made us hungry.

"Lord, thank You for these children and for their snack," Grampa prayed. "Help them to love You."

"Do you always pray for snacks?" I asked.

"Why not?" said Grampa. "Aren't you thankful for snacks?"

"Well, yes," I said. "But at home we usually just pray before meals."

"That's fine," said Grampa. "I just like to pray."

Jake and I had a fine snack. When we were finished, we colored on the magic tablecloth.

I got bored before Jake, so I went hunting for the lost owls again. I went to Grampa's room and looked under his bed. Nothing was there.

I opened his closet. It was a funny closet because it didn't have a back wall. If you pushed through Grampa's clothes, you ended up in the closet to my room.

When I first discovered the closet that was really two closets, I didn't tell Jake. I wanted to trick her. I went into my room and came out Grampa's.

"How did you do that?" she asked. "Did you climb out your window and in Grampa's?"

I just smiled and kept my secret. But the next time I thought I'd trick her, she caught me coming out of the closet!

Now I looked all around the floor on Grampa's side of the closet. I pushed through his clothes to my side and opened my door. I stepped into my room. I hadn't seen anything but clothes.

I went back to Grampa's room. I stood and looked up at the top shelf of his closet. I knew I couldn't see what was there, but that was all right. The top shelf was full of all the books that held his coin collection.

It was special when he took some of his coin books down.

"See this old dime, Scooter?" he'd say. "It was given to me by my father. And look at this one, Jake. Gramma found it on the sidewalk when she dropped her glove. See that little mark? That means it's very rare."

I looked up at Grampa's top shelf and felt cold all over.

Not one coin book was up there.

CHAPTER
9

I ran down to the kitchen. Jake was still coloring on the tablecloth. I grabbed the crayon from her hand.

"Come with me," I said. "I've got to talk to you."

"Scooter! Don't grab! It's rude." She took her crayon back and drew some more.

"Jake, you've got to come with me," I said.

"Go away," she said.

I put my hand on her drawing.

"Stop it, Scooter," she said. Then she looked up and saw my face, and she knew I was upset.

"What's wrong?"

"Shhh," I said. "Don't upset Gramma. Come with me."

We ran upstairs and into Grampa's room. I showed her the empty shelf.

"What does it mean?" she asked.

I shook my head. "I don't know. Grampa

wouldn't hide his whole coin collection, would he?"

"I don't think so," said Jake. "I mean, why would he? And where would he hide it if he did?"

"Another closet?" I said.

"That doesn't make sense," Jake said.

I agreed. "But if he's taking and hiding things, can we expect it to make sense?"

Because we couldn't think of anything else to do, we looked in all the closets. We looked in all the bedrooms. We looked in the upstairs hall. We went downstairs and looked in the front hall. Then we went to the back hall.

I looked up at the shelf of this closet. I saw a couple of hats and a scarf. Fingers from a pair of gloves hung over the edge. There were no coin books.

We started for the basement to look down there, when I remembered something. I rushed back to the closet.

"Jake," I said. "It's gone! The silver pitcher that was on the top shelf is gone! It was there just this morning!"

CHAPTER 10

"What pitcher?" said Gramma. She had come into the hall behind us.

"The silver one that you pour coffee out of on Christmas," I said. I pointed to the top shelf. "It was there."

"It doesn't belong up there," Gramma said. "It's kept in the sideboard in the dining room." Gramma went back to the kitchen, talking to herself. "As if I'd keep something that good in the back hall closet."

"It was there," I said.

"So where is it now?" Jake said.

We went to the dining room. Jake opened the door of the sideboard, and we looked in.

Gramma has a big silver tray that she gets out on very special days like Christmas. On the big tray she puts a tall pitcher that holds coffee and a short, fat one that holds tea. There are also a little cream

pitcher and a sugar bowl.

Mom thinks the tray and pitchers are wonderful.

"Oh, Gramma," she says. "You're so lucky to have such beautiful things."

"I thank God for them all the time," Gramma answers.

Now Jake and I looked and looked, but it was always the same. All those beautiful things were gone.

We looked at each other.

"Grampa wouldn't hide the silver things," Jake said. "Would he?"

"I don't think so," I said. "And I don't think he'd hide his coins either."

"How many things do we know are missing?" Jake asked.

"The little owl with the silver feet and eyes," I said. "And the owl picture. Grampa's coin collection. The silver coffeepot and teapot and stuff. And the stone chessmen."

"Wow," said Jake. "I didn't know that many things were missing."

I was surprised myself.

"I wonder how many other things are missing," Jake said.

"You mean things we haven't discovered yet?" I shook my head. "I don't know. We'd better look."

Very carefully we went around the dining room, then the living room.

"What are you two doing?" Grampa asked. He was sitting in his favorite chair, reading the newspaper.

"Just looking at stuff," I said.

Finally Jake and I went out and sat on the front steps.

"The pretty painted dish in the dining room is missing," Jake said.

"So is the statue of the girl in the pink dress and big hat," I said.

"The candy dish that usually sits on the sideboard is gone," said Jake.

"And I didn't see the blue vase with the white flowers that should be on the table by the sofa."

I liked that vase. When Jake and I picked wildflowers for Gramma she usually put them in it.

Jake and I looked at each other. What in the world was going on?

"There's only one possible answer," said Jake.

I nodded. "Someone is stealing things."

We sat and thought and thought.

"He must come in while Gramma and Grampa are out," I said.

"But Old Henry is usually here," Jake said.

"Anybody could come into the house with Old Henry here," I said. "Old Henry is so old and deaf and slow. He'd never hear anyone. And if he did, he'd be too tired to do anything."

"I guess that's true," Jake said.

"I think someone came in today while we were at the lake."

Jake nodded. "So what should we do about it?"

"I guess we should tell Gramma and Grampa," I said.

"It's going to make them very sad," Jake said.

We went back inside and to the kitchen.

"Gramma," we said, "can you come into the living room a minute? We need to talk to you and Grampa."

"Oh, I don't think I can come now," Gramma said. "I'm busy with dinner."

"Please," we said. "You have to come now."

Gramma looked at us. Our faces showed her we were upset.

"What's wrong, sweethearts?" she asked.

"Come into the living room," we said. "We want to tell you and Grampa at the same time."

Gramma put a lid on the pan she was cooking in and turned the heat down. She came to the living room with us.

"Grampa," we said, "put your newspaper down for a minute, please."

"Just a second," he said. "I'm reading a very good story."

"Please, Grampa. Now," we said.

He put his paper down and looked at us. Then he folded his paper and put it on the floor.

"Someone has been stealing a lot of your things," I said.

"What?" said Grampa.

"Someone has been stealing your things."

"Like the owls?" Grampa asked.

Jake and I both said, "Yes."

"Oh, no!" said Gramma.

"How wonderful!" exclaimed Grampa.

CHAPTER 12

Gramma, Jake, and I stared at Grampa.

"How can you say it's wonderful?" Gramma asked.

"Of course it's very bad," said Grampa. "But if someone is stealing things, then I'm not the problem. I'm not taking them. I'm not hiding them. I'm not forgetting them." He smiled a big, happy grin. "I'm all right!"

Gramma, Jake, and I nodded. Now we understood why he was happy.

"I'm so glad you're all right, my dear," Gramma said. She got up and hugged Grampa. "I'm very happy for you."

They smiled at each other for a minute. Then Gramma started to cry.

"But who would steal from us?" she asked. "And what did they steal?"

Jake and I told them.

"My little girl in the pink dress?" Gramma cried harder.

"My chessmen? My coins?" Grampa sounded angry.

"You ought to look around," I said. "There may be more things that Jake and I didn't notice."

We walked around the house with Gramma and Grampa as they looked.

"My gold necklace," said Gramma.

"And my gold tie pin," said Grampa.

"Two new green towels," said Gramma. "And the washcloths that went with them."

"A very old clock," said Grampa.

"The little owl we got on vacation," Gramma said.

"The big owl I got you for your birthday," Grampa said.

It was a sad time. Gramma wanted to write everything down on a list. She was crying so hard she couldn't write.

"I'll write for you," Jake said. "You can spell for me if I don't know the words."

"Why would someone do this?" asked Gramma.

"That's easy," I said. "All the things are pretty. Some of them are worth lots of money."

"Like my coins," said Grampa.

"And my silver pitchers," said Gramma.

"But who would do it?" asked Grampa. "Who would want to hurt us like this?"

"I'm afraid that's easy too," I said.

"It is?" Jake said.

"It is?" Gramma and Grampa said.

I nodded. "Sure it is," I said. "I know who did it."

CHAPTER 13

A sudden noise came from the dining room. It sounded as though someone had bumped into the house.

"What was that?" asked Gramma. She was jumpy because she was upset.

"I don't know," said Grampa. He looked concerned. "We'd better check."

Even Old Henry woke up and waddled behind us. We all went quickly to the dining room. Everything looked fine to me.

"Maybe the noise came from outside," Grampa said.

We crowded around and looked out the window. All we saw was the back side of the hedge and then the lawn and then the street. No one was there.

Then suddenly Freddie was there, standing between the house and the hedge. He had been bent over, and when he stood up, there he was.

"Freddie," Gramma said, shocked. "What are

you doing outside my window?"

"Checking the hose again?" I asked.

"What?" said Freddie. "Oh, yes. The hose. Yes, I was checking it. It's okay."

"You've been checking that area a lot today, haven't you?" I asked.

"What do you mean?" Freddie said.

"You had this window open this morning," I said. "I saw you leaning out."

"So?" said Freddie. "Taking care of the windows is part of my job."

"You were working on the hedge here when we came home from the lake," I said.

"As I said, I was checking the hose," Freddie said.

"And you're checking the hose now?" I asked.

"Sure," said Freddie. "I've already said that, too."

"The hose isn't there, Freddie," said Grampa. "It's on the side of the house. You can't be checking it."

"The hedge," said Freddie. He was talking fast. "I'm checking the hedge. The hedge is part of my job."

"By the way, Freddie," I asked. "Why do you have your hands behind your back? What do you have in them?"

CHAPTER 14

"I don't have anything in my hands," Freddie said.

"Let's see," I said. "Come on. Let's see."

Suddenly Freddie held up empty hands.

I blinked, surprised. I was sure he'd have the silver pitcher. I had it all figured out.

First he had taken it from Gramma's sideboard.

I surprised him before he got it out of the house.

He put it in the closet so I wouldn't know he was taking it.

While I got Gramma's wash for her, he put the pitcher out the window behind the hedge.

When we went to the lake, he came back for it. We came home before he got it.

He thought we were eating dinner in the kitchen, so he came back again to get it.

But if his hands were empty, where was the pitcher?

Grampa looked at Freddie. "Did you take any of our things?" he asked. He didn't want Freddie to be the thief.

"You're my friends," said Freddie. "Would I take things from friends?"

While they talked, I had an idea. I ran outside. On my way I grabbed Grampa's cane. I went to where Freddie was. I fell to my knees and looked under the hedge. There, lying in the dirt, was Gramma's silver coffeepot.

"It's there!" I yelled. "He was stealing it!"

Freddie jumped and spun around. I guess he wanted to break through the hedge and run away. Sadly for him, he stepped on the silver pot. It rolled underneath him, and he went flying. He fell hard. I felt the ground shake when he hit. He just lay there.

"I'm calling 911," yelled Jake. "We need the police!" And she ran for the phone.

Grampa hurried outside and around the side of the house. He hurried back dragging the hose.

Gramma ran to the kitchen and then out front carrying her broom.

Jake rushed out. "I called the police! They're coming." In her hand she had a heavy frying pan.

Even Old Henry waddled out and stood beside

Grampa, growling.
When Freddie finally got to his feet, he was surrounded by the five of us with our cane, hose, broom, frying pan, and growl. I was glad the police got there before we had to use any of them.

CHAPTER

15

When Mom and Dad got back from their little vacation, we told them about our big adventure.

"Oh, Grampa," said Dad. "I'm sorry. I know you really liked Freddie."

Grampa was sad. "I did. I trusted him. Gramma made him cookies lots of times. He and I talked and joked. We thought he was our friend."

"I didn't know before that stealing hurts people inside more than it hurts them outside," said Jake. "It's very cruel."

"That's right," said Gramma. "I'm glad to have my things back, but they're only things. It's my heart that hurts because a friend wasn't really a friend."

"He stole your kindness as well as your things," I said. "Instead of doing good the way the Bible says, he did bad."

Old Henry walked over to Gramma. He put his

head on her knee.

"Look at him," said Mom. "He wants you to know that we still love you, Gramma."

"Dear God," prayed Grampa, "help us to remember to do good to all. We don't want to make poor choices, the way Freddie did. And keep Scooter and Jake safe until they come visit us again."

We walked to our car and climbed in.

"I have one last thing for you," said Gramma. She held out a bag.

I opened it. "Popcorn for the trip home," I said. "Thanks, Gramma. You've been doing good."